Made in the USA
Thornton, CO
10/18/22 10:00:11

5449f6cb-235c-4a52-83c7-5ee06568e96cR01